PENGUINS:

Theme Unit
Developed in Cooperation with
P.R.B.O. International
Biological Research

by Robin Bernard

SCHOLASTIC
PROFESSIONAL BOOKS

NEW YORK ◆ TORONTO ◆ LONDON ◆ AUCKLAND ◆ SYDNEY

DEDICATION

*F*or Jer, who made all things possible. Usingizi m'zuri.

ACKNOWLEDGMENTS

*M*y gratitude to Dr. David Ainley for proofreading this
manuscript, for his fine photographs, and most of all
for answering my questions with clarity and patience; thanks
also to Terry Cooper for the opportunity to wallow in penguins;
to Diane Rosen for helping me understand what fascinates
second graders; to Liza Schafer for being the kind of editor I've
always wanted; and as always, and in all ways, to JL.

Cover design by Vincent Ceci

Book design by Jo-Ann Rosiello Design, NYC

Penguin illustrations by Robin Bernard

Technical illustrations by Jo-Ann Rosiello

Photos by David Ainley

ISBN 0-590-49639-5

TABLE ◆ OF ◆ CONTENTS

P.R.B.O. International Biological Research (also known as Point Reyes Bird Observatory) had its start in 1965. It is located in Stinson Beach, 15 miles north of San Francisco, California. Overall, P.R.B.O. strives to provide credible, scientifically based guidance for environmental stewardship in the Pacific Rim. Its research emphasizes long-term ecological studies of birds and their terrestrial, wetland, and marine habitats. P.R.B.O. is a non-advocacy, membership-supported research and educational organization. Additional funds come from donations of members, corporations, private foundations, as well as grants and contracts from state and federal agencies. Its Antarctic penguin work was supported by the National Science Foundation.

Projects on marine birds at P.R.B.O. have spanned the length and breadth of the Pacific Ocean. P.R.B.O. is custodian of the Farallon Island National Wildlife Refuge, home to one of the most diverse and largest marine avifaunas on the North American Pacific coast. Guarding these breeding colonies so close to one of the world's largest coastal metropolitan areas is no small task but recent years have seen significant recovery by several Farallon populations. Other sites where P.R.B.O. investigates the land-based portion of seabird lives include Kauai, in the Hawaiian Islands, and Ross Island, in the Ross Sea, Antarctica. Investigations of the marine side to seabirds take place on oceanographic cruises to the California Current offshore of central California; the equatorial Pacific between the Galápagos and Hawaiian islands; and in the Southern Ocean, south of Pacific waters.

P.R.B.O.'s marine studies investigate the place of birds among other vertebrates (including man) in marine food webs. Besides expanding our appreciation of marine systems and working to restore the Farallones, P.R.B.O. research has played an important role in establishing the Ecosystem Monitoring Program of the Convention of Antarctic Marine Living Resources, an international treaty; regulating the use of gill nets (to avoid catching non-target species) in California and Alaskan waters; listing the California population of the Stellar Sea Lion as "threatened" under the Endangered Species Act and protection of the White Shark in California (both results of Farallon projects); establishing guidelines for ocean disposal of material dredged from coastal harbors; and assessing wildlife damage and recovery from oil spills in Alaska, California, and Antarctica. A current P.R.B.O. project is directed toward reducing mortality among endangered, nocturnal seabirds that collide with utility structures on Kauai.

Marine research was initiated at P.R.B.O. in 1971 by David Ainley, Program Director for Marine Studies. Currently, seven P.R.B.O. staff members and a host of volunteers are involved in the marine work.

Getting to Know Penguins

Have Feathers, Don't Fly

There are many flightless birds: ostriches, kiwis, cormorants, rails, and even a parrot. Yet none seem to capture our imagination and affection the way penguins do. This book is designed to introduce your students to the special abilities and behaviors of penguins through a series of fun-filled learning activities. Some of the words used in the students' material may be new to the children. These are defined in the text, and more thoroughly in the Glossary.

Deep Freeze

Antarctica: the coldest place on earth? Not always. Fossils and coal deposits reveal that Antarctica was once warm and green. At that time, the continent was located farther to the north than it is now. There were forests, flowers, insects, and later, penguins! Of all the types of birds we know, penguins are among the oldest, having been on earth for more than 40 million years.

When the Antarctic continent shifted southward to the polar region, it became locked in an icy grip. Over a long period of time, penguins, which had long been at home in temperate seas, adapted in ways that made it possible for them to survive in frigid conditions.

When a polar penguin dives into Antarctic waters, it swims comfortably in temperatures that would kill a human within minutes. A penguin is protected by a thick layer of blubber and a dense undercoat of downy feathers that trap its body heat. Topping it off is a waterproof coat made of overlapping feathers which provides additional protection in the harsh environment.

Not All Penguins Are Polar

Penguins make their homes in cool waters that are nutrient rich—conditions prevalent in both the Southern and Northern Hemisphere. However, no penguins venture north of the Equator and not all penguins live in the *polar* region. Surprisingly, cool waters exist close to the Equator in the South Pacific Ocean. Some penguins nest in forested areas with ferns, shrubs, and pastures; others nest where cacti grow! In all cases, because a penguin, by swimming, can cover much less area in search of food than a seabird can by flying, productive waters, and abundant food must exist close to nesting areas.

What's So Special About Penguins?

We all recognize penguins when we see them, but if we look at their individual physical characteristics, it's easy to understand how specific adaptations helped them survive. A penguin's beak, for instance, is used for:

◆ breathing
◆ catching food
◆ feeding its chicks
◆ preening its feathers
◆ carrying nesting material
◆ protecting itself and its young.

Even the penguin's coloring is multi-purpose. Besides allowing penguins to recognize each other, the tuxedo that is so obvious on shore becomes instant camouflage in the water. The penguin's dark back makes it hard for a predator to see it from above, and the white belly, when viewed from below, blends with the light at the water's surface.

WHAT'S SO SPECIAL ABOUT PENGUINS? MINI-BOOK:

Before starting the Mini-Book project, show your students a picture of a penguin and ask them to name its parts: feet, beak, flippers (wings), feathers, etc.

Explain that each of these parts has more than one function. Your students will become familiar with penguins' special abilities by making and reading the mini-book on the following pages.

Make double-sided copies of pages 9 and 10, being careful not to invert the picture on the reverse side. Students can assemble their books by following these directions:

1. Cut along solid line to make flap.
2. Fold page in half along dashed line that runs full width of page so that the title page and penguin features are visible on outside.
3. Fold in half again along the dashed line that runs across top of title page.
4. Fold in half a third time along dashed line to left of title page.
5. Finished book will look like this:

Extension Activity:

After allowing time for students to read and share their books, invite them to tell what parts of their bodies perform functions similar to penguins' parts. For example: *Penguins' wings help them swim in water; our arms help us swim in water.* Now have students use their penguin books as models to make books about themselves: What's So Special About (student's name). Students might tell about how they use their hands, arms, legs, feet, eyes, ears, and mouths.

PENGUIN MOBILE:

Make double-sided copies of pages 11 and 12. There are five kinds of penguins for your students to cut out and assemble into mobiles. Before they begin, ask students to study the penguins carefully and give each a nickname. (They can write the nicknames in the spaces above the species' names.) The nicknames can be based on physical traits and/or the real name—"Charlie-Chinstrap," for instance, or "Rocky." This exercise will help students remember these particular species, and at the same time learn what characteristics "birders" look for when identifying any species, such as eye-rings, stripes, crests, beak shape, etc.

Extension Activity:

Ask students to share names of birds they are familiar with, such as robin, duck, owl, or pigeon. List bird names on the board and record students' descriptions of each. Use a bird guide to check information and to learn more about the identifying characteristics of each bird.

Invite students to apply what they learn about using characteristics to identify birds. Ask: *What information could someone use to identify you?* Have students write and illustrate guide book entries about their distinguishing characteristics. Students might include information about size, behaviors, habitats, interests, sounds, songs, and so on. Put students' pages together to make a class Pocket Guide to People.

IN PRAISE OF PENGUINS:

The poem on page 14 praises penguins with affection and humorous images based on actual penguin biology and behavior. Students can take turns reading parts of it aloud before writing and illustrating their own penguin poems. They may want to use rhymes from the word block to the right or invent their own. You might assemble students' illustrated poems into a class Big Book of Penguins. (Young children not yet able to write can dictate their poems to be illustrated and assembled as above.)

**NICE – ICE
WINGS – THINGS
BOLD – COLD
FLY – SKY
HUDDLE – CUDDLE
WISH – FISH
BILL – KRILL
SEAL – MEAL
WEATHER – FEATHER
SLIDE – RIDE**

What's So Special About PENGUINS

WINGS

Penguins use their wings like flippers to swim. Their wings also make good snow paddles.

FEATHERS

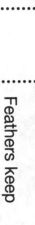

Feathers keep penguins warm and dry. Their feathers grow so close together, they look like fur!

TAIL

In the water, penguins' tails act like rudders. On land, their tails make good props.

FEET

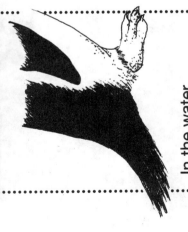

Penguins' webbed feet are wide and strong. They can steer and brake.

Put the parts together and you have a special bird!

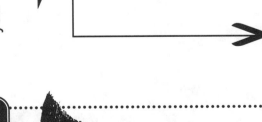

BEAK

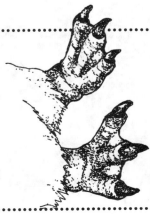

Penguins' beaks have sharp edges. Rough "spines" inside their beaks help penguins hold slippery fish.

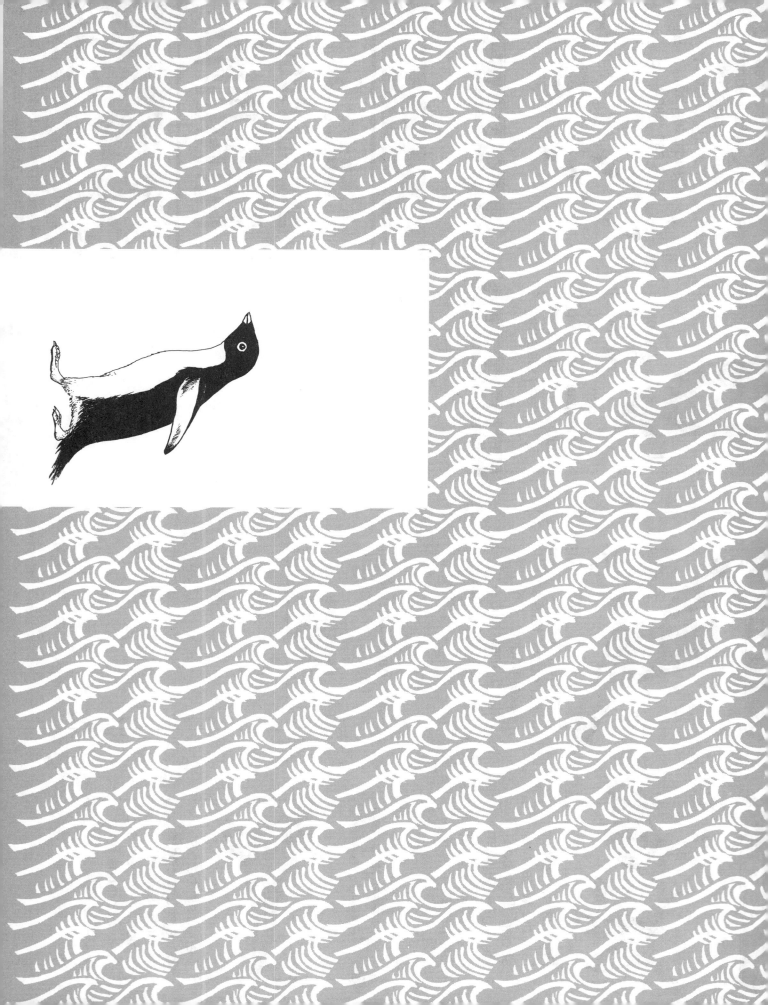

PENGUIN FRIENDS MOBILE

LITTLE BLUE

CHINSTRAP

What You Need:
◆ scissors   ◆ hole punch
◆ string   ◆ wire hanger

What You Do:
1. Cut out the pictures along the dashed lines.
2. Use a hole punch to cut out the circles.
3. Cut five pieces of string—each one a different length.
4. Tie a piece of string through each of the holes.
5. Tie the other end of each piece to the hanger.
6. Hang your penguin mobile where everyone can see it!

ROCKHOPPER

ADÉLIE

GALÁPAGOS

LITTLE BLUE

CHINSTRAP

GALÁPAGOS

ADÉLIE

ROCKHOPPER

12

PENGUIN FRIENDS MOBILE

When you're finished making your mobile, use it to answer these questions:

1. Look at the Chinstrap. How do you think this penguin got its name?

_____

2. What eye markings make the Adélie special?

_____

3. Because it is so small, one of the penguins is also known as the "fairy penguin." Which one do you think it is?

_____

4. What makes the Rockhopper penguin look different?

_____

5. What marking does the Galápagos penguin have on its chest that the others don't ?

_____

6. What nicknames did you give the penguins?

Rockhopper_____

Galápagos_____

Little Blue_____

Adélie_____

Chinstrap_____

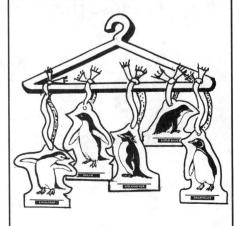

In Praise of Penguins

These funny birds in fancy clothes
may waddle in the snow,
but when they reach the icy sea
just watch how fast they go!

Their song sounds like a donkey's bray,
they cannot soar or fly,
yet penguins manage very well,
and let me tell you why....

Their feathers keep out water,
their blubber keeps out cold,
their wings make perfect paddles
because they do not fold!

Their tails are good for steering,
they brake with both their feet—
So tell me now, from all you've heard,...
Aren't penguins NEAT?

Identifying Penguins

If you've only seen one, you've definitely not seen them all! While the Adélie may be the image that comes to mind when most of us think of penguins, each of the 18 species of penguins has its own physical characteristics, abilities, and behavior patterns. Being able to recognize and name a species is often the first step a child takes onto a path of wonderful discoveries. Penguins can be identified by other penguins (and people) by markings on their heads and necks, the parts that are visible above the water's surface when they're swimming. Although there are other differences—size, color of the feet, some spotting on the chest—the heads are the primary identification factor. This is why they're shown in detail on the Penguin Profile cards. The cards show 12 kinds of penguins to introduce to your students, all interesting and easy to identify.

PENGUIN PROFILE CARDS:

The 12 cards on pages 17 to 22 will help your students understand how penguin species differ in terms of size, habitats, markings, and abilities. Reproduce and distribute the sheets, and have children cut, paste, and assemble them. After students read the information on each card and look at the illustrations, ask them to describe some penguin traits they think are especially interesting. They can use the information on the cards with the suggested activities below, and with the map skills activity in Penguins on the Move, page 32.

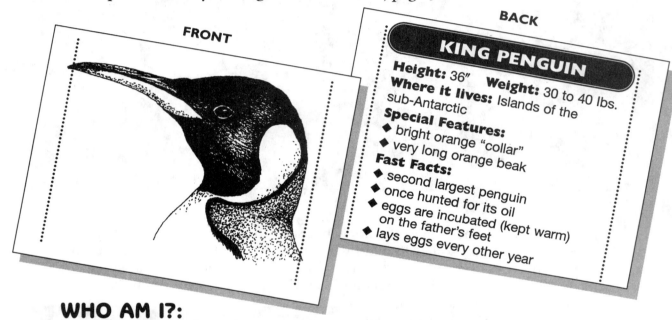

FRONT

BACK

KING PENGUIN

Height: 36"   **Weight:** 30 to 40 lbs.
Where it lives: Islands of the sub-Antarctic

Special Features:
◆ bright orange "collar"
◆ very long orange beak

Fast Facts:
◆ second largest penguin
◆ once hunted for its oil
◆ eggs are incubated (kept warm) on the father's feet
◆ lays eggs every other year

WHO AM I?:

The two spinner games on page 23 are based on Penguin Profile Cards information. After cutting and assembling both spinners, divide the class into pairs of students and have each pair lay out one set of cards between them so that the penguin illustrations are face up. Ask them to take turns spinning and trying to name the penguin described in the segment the spinner indicates. After selecting the picture of the penguin they think is correct, they can then check their answers by turning the card over. If they're right, they keep the card. If they're wrong, the card is flipped back over. The player with the most cards wins. (Note: If the spinner lands on a previously identified penguin, the player spins again.)

STAND UP BIRDS:

In the activity on pages 24 and 25 students will make a bar graph of penguin sizes. Distribute copies to your students and ask them to use their Profile Cards to find each penguin's height. After entering the information, students can color the columns and use their graph to answer the questions.

PENGUIN PROFILES

The cards on these six pages will help you learn more about penguins. To make them, cut along solid lines, then fold them along the dashed line. Tape or paste the front and back of each card together.

AFRICAN PENGUIN

Height: 27" **Weight:** 7 to 11 lbs.

Where it lives: island off South African coast

Special Features:
◆ wide face stripe
◆ sounds like a donkey
◆ bare skin on forehead

Fast Facts:
◆ endangered species
◆ digs burrows in sand with its beak
◆ lays eggs twice each year

ADÉLIE PENGUIN

Height: 28" **Weight:** 8 to 14 lbs.

Where it lives: Antarctica

Special Features:
◆ white eye-ring
◆ feathers cover most of its beak
◆ very long tail

Fast Facts:
◆ builds nests of pebbles
◆ its chick grows the fastest

EMPEROR PENGUIN

Height: 45" **Weight:** 70 to 90 lbs.

Where it lives: on Antarctic ice

Special Features:
- yellow patches on upper chest and on each side of its head
- purple beak

Fast Facts:
- the largest penguin
- it can dive nearly 900 feet
- the egg is incubated (kept warm) on the father's feet
- lays eggs during winter

CHINSTRAP PENGUIN

Height: 28" **Weight:** 9 to 14 lbs.

Where it lives: Antarctic peninsula and islands

Special Features:
- thin black line under its chin

Fast Facts:
- considered the boldest penguin
- eats mostly krill (tiny shrimp-like animals)
- more likely to fight than other penguins

GENTOO PENGUIN

Height: 32" **Weight:** 10 to 19 lbs.

Where it lives: Antarctic peninsula and sub-Antarctic islands

Special Features:
- white patch on head
- red bill
- orange feet

Fast Facts:
- fastest swimming penguin
- builds nests of old bones and feathers that have molted (fallen out)

GALÁPAGOS PENGUIN

Height: 21" **Weight:** 4 to 6 lbs.

Where it lives: near the Equator on the Galápagos Islands, further north than any other penguin

Special Features:
- double chest band
- bare skin around eyes

Fast Facts:
- endangered species
- lives among land crabs and marine iguanas
- smallest tropical penguin

LITTLE BLUE PENGUIN

Height: 15" **Weight:** 2 to 4 lbs.

Where it lives: islands off southern Australia and New Zealand

Special Features:
◆ gray-blue "tuxedo"

Fast Facts:
◆ smallest penguin
◆ dips head before diving
◆ spends nights in burrows
◆ makes barking and quacking sounds

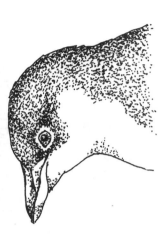

KING PENGUIN

Height: 36" **Weight:** 30 to 40 lbs.

Where it lives: Islands of the sub-Antarctic

Special Features:
◆ bright orange "collar"
◆ very long orange beak

Fast Facts:
◆ second largest penguin
◆ once hunted for its oil
◆ eggs are incubated (kept warm) on the father's feet
◆ lays eggs every other year

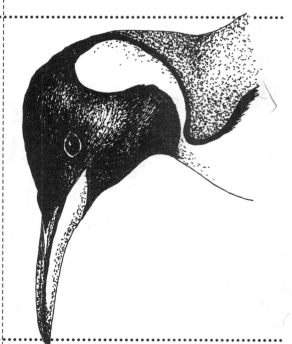

ROCKHOPPER PENGUIN

Height: 22"   **Weight:** 5 to 10 lbs.

Where it lives: sub-Antarctic, Falkland Islands

Special Features:
◆ crest
◆ yellow eyebrows and plumes
◆ red beak and red eyes

Fast Facts:
◆ seems to "pop" out of the water onto rocks
◆ hops from boulder to boulder
◆ lives in huge colonies (groups)

MAGELLANIC PENGUIN

Height: 28"   **Weight:** 10 to 15 lbs.

Where it lives: coastal areas of Chile, Argentina, Falkland Islands

Special Features:
◆ two black chest bands
◆ brays, moos, and cackles

Fast Facts:
◆ digs burrows in sand or clay
◆ hunted by orcas (killer whales) and kelp gulls

YELLOW-EYED PENGUIN

Height: 26" **Weight:** 9 to 14 lbs.

Where it lives: southern New Zealand, Auckland, Campbell, and Enderby Islands

Special Features:
- yellow eyes and crown

Fast Facts:
- shy, comes ashore at night
- nests under rocks and roots
- shares island with rabbits
- mates for life

ROYAL PENGUIN

Height: 28" **Weight:** 11 to 16 lbs.

Where it lives: Macquerie Island, the southernmost "green" island in the world

Special Features:
- large red bill
- floppy yellow crest

Fast Facts:
- shares island with elephant seals
- has muddy nesting sites
- lays two eggs, hatches only one chick

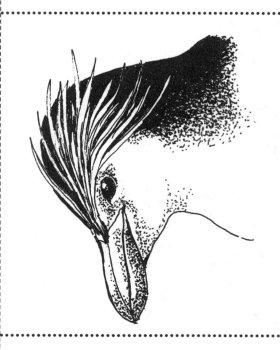

WHO AM I ?

Cut out each spinner. Open a paperclip to form an "S" shape. Use a brass fastener to attach one end of the "S" shape to the center of each spinner, as shown.

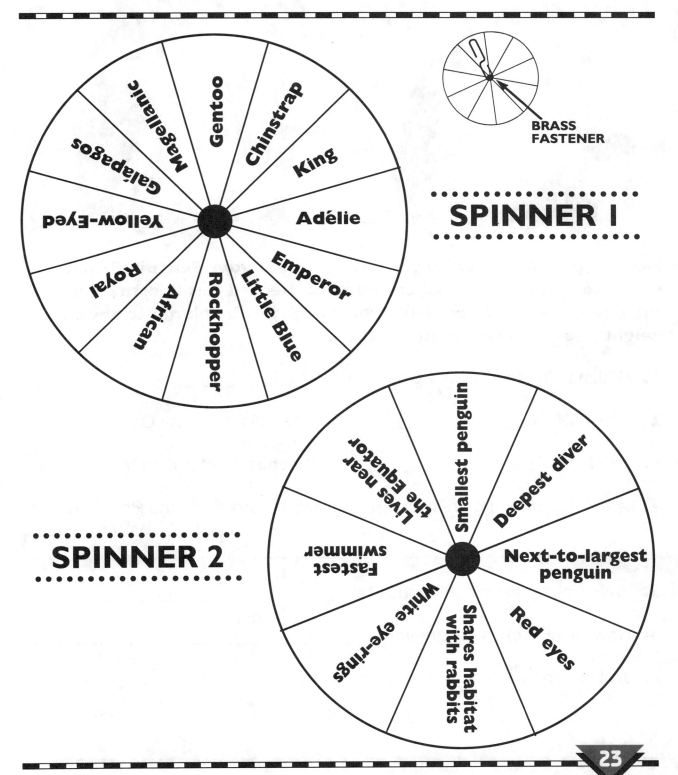

BRASS FASTENER

SPINNER 1

Spinner 1 labels: Gentoo, Chinstrap, King, Adélie, Emperor, Little Blue, Rockhopper, African, Royal, Yellow-Eyed, Galápagos, Magellanic

SPINNER 2

Spinner 2 labels: Smallest penguin, Deepest diver, Next-to-largest penguin, Red eyes, Shares habitat with rabbits, White eye-rings, Fastest swimmer, Lives near the Equator

STAND UP BIRDS

How do penguins measure up? First look at your Penguin Profile Cards to find out how tall each one is. Record this information on the chart (see next page) and color each bird's column to show its height. Now you can compare them.

1. Which is the third tallest penguin?_____

2. The Adélie is _____ inches taller than the Galápagos.

3. The Little Blue is _____ inches shorter than the Emperor.

4. Is the African penguin closer in height to the Adélie or the Rockhopper?

_____

5. Which penguins are 28 inches tall? _____

6. How many inches tall are you? _____

7. Which penguin is closest to your height? _____

Name _____

	Galápagos	King	Yellow-Eyed	Adélie	Magellanic	Gentoo	Emperor	African	Rock-Hopper	Royal	Little Blue	Chinstrap

INCHES

45
40
35
30
25
20
15
10
5
0

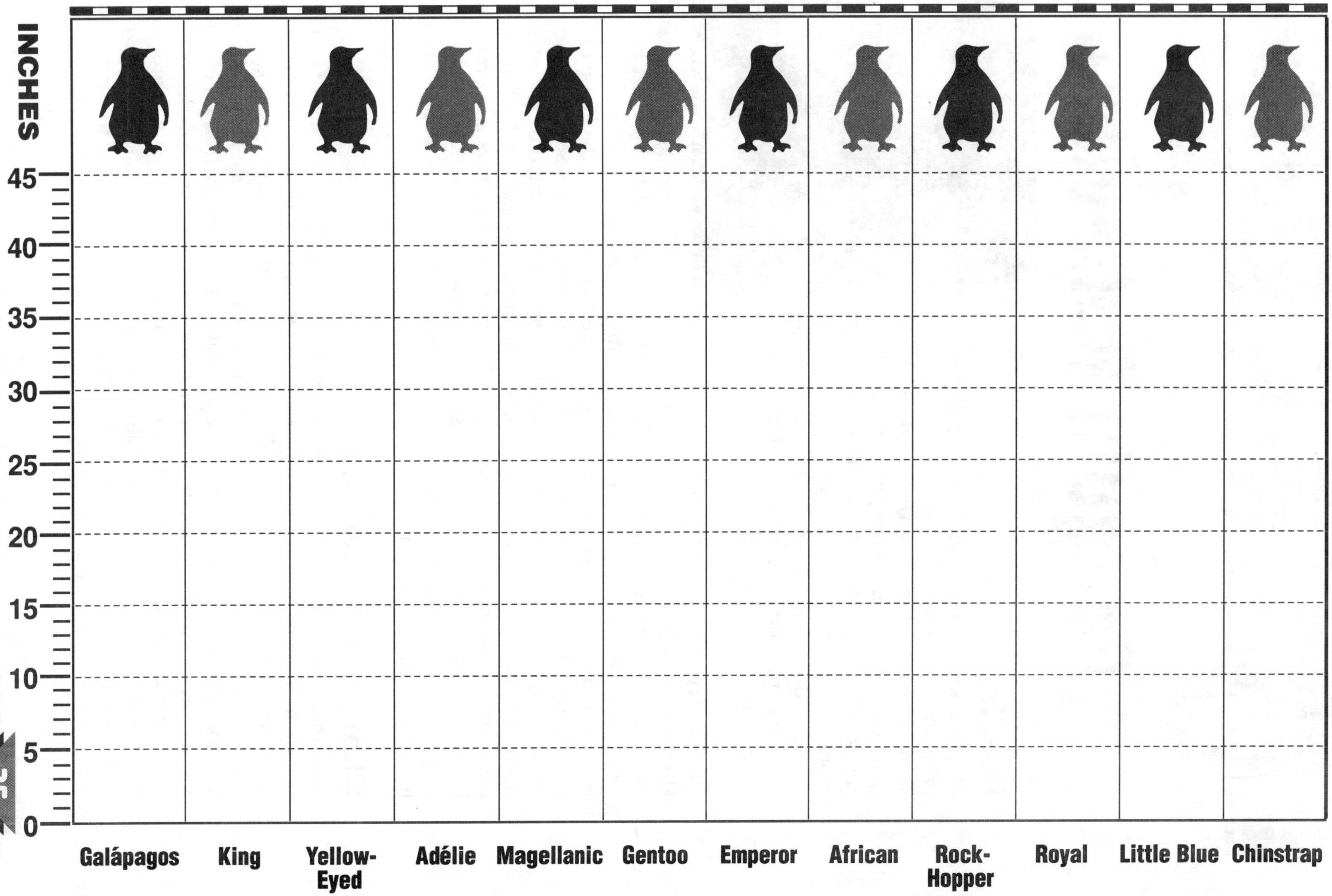

Penguin Behavior

Feeding

All penguins (except chicks whose parents bring them food) hunt in the water, usually swimming several miles to their feeding grounds. Emperor and King penguins find krill and squid in the darkness of deep water, while other species feed closer to the surface. Penguins drink both fresh and salt water (Antarctic penguins eat snow), and can release excess salt from glands above their eyes.

Breeding

Most penguins lay eggs once a year, although some of the tropical species such as the Galápagos may breed twice a year if food is plentiful enough. Adélies cross many miles of sea ice to return to their Antarctic nesting sites, where courtship is noisy and nest-building material (small stones) is frequently the cause of squabbling. Biologists have recently noted that female Adélies select a mate with a proven ability to fast, or one who has the potential (indicated by size and deep voice) to help incubate an egg despite extreme hunger. While Adélies construct pebble nests, to which they add some molted feathers and even old bones, the more tropical penguins use twigs, moss, and grass. Kings and Emperors have no nests, but incubate their eggs on their feet—the best nesting material available to them.

Change of Outerwear

Very young penguins look so unlike their parents that the first scientists who saw them thought they were a different species, and called them "Woolly penguins." After they shed their baby feathers, however, the chicks look more like the adults. All birds shed their feathers at least once a year, but flying birds only lose a few at a time, or they'd be grounded. Penguins shed all their feathers at once (in two to five weeks), an event known as "catastrophic molting." While the new feathers push the old ones out, the birds look scruffy and ungroomed. Because they aren't waterproof while they molt, penguins can't go in the water—so they're not only grounded, they're beached, and have to survive on layers of fat acquired prior to molting.

Emperor on Ice

The largest penguin lives in the coldest climate on earth, spending its life in frigid ocean water or on sea ice where temperatures may drop to –76˚ F! The Emperor is also the only penguin that goes without food for three months at a time. The fast begins when the Emperors return to land from the sea in March and April (Antarctic autumn). A month passes by the time courtship and breeding are over and the female lays her single egg in the darkness of the Antarctic night. During all this time, the penguins are out of the water, so they can't eat. They live on their own body fat and eat snow for water. Shortly after the egg is laid, the female returns to the ocean to feed, leaving her mate to incubate the egg. Using his beak, he carefully rolls the egg onto the top of his feet. He tucks it under the warm brood patch on his lower belly, and stands huddled with other fathers-to-be in large groups.

He shuffles around in the dark for two more months, without eating, in bitter cold temperatures and blizzards! When the egg hatches, at about sunrise some-time in September, the mother returns and takes over parenting duties. By this time, the male has slimmed down, having lost about 35 pounds. As hungry as he is, after transferring the chick to his mate's feet, he stays around for another day or two before heading for the sea. When he returns a few weeks later he's fat again, full of krill, squid, and fish. The parents then take turns carrying the tiny chick on their feet, and bringing it food. After five and a half months the young penguin takes its first plunge, just when the ocean has the greatest amount of krill and squid.

Hans Reinhard/Bruce Coleman Inc.

GROWING UP:

Students will enjoy following the development of an Adélie penguin (considered the most "penguiny" penguin) by making the mini-book on pages 29 and 30. Make double-sided photocopies of the pages, being careful not to invert the reverse side of the page. Distribute a copy to each student. They can make their books by following these directions:

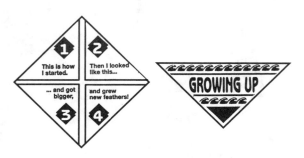

1. Cut along the solid line and discard strip.

2. Fold all four corners along the dashed lines and into the center covering the pictures.

3. Fold in half along the dashed line to form a triangle. The completed mini-book will have "Growing Up" on the cover.

Extension Activity:

After younger students make and color their Growing Up books, you might follow up with a simple sequencing activity. Using a copy of page 30, cut apart the pictures. Let students take turns using their completed books to put the pictures in order. Invite pre-readers to tell the story in their own words.

EMPEROR FOR A DAY:

Reproduce copies of page 31 and distribute to each student. By trying to balance an "egg" on their feet, students can have fun acting out an important task performed by male Emperor penguins. Walking (shuffling) will be a little difficult without penguin feet or a brood patch but on the plus side is the fact that the human Emperors aren't on sheet ice, in the dark, or trying to remain upright in icy winds and snow storms!

Extension Activity:

How do other animals carry their babies? The following questions can help guide your discussion.

◆ How do you think lions and other cats carry their cubs from place to place? (in their mouths)

◆ How do you think kangaroos carry their babies? (in their pouches)

◆ Can you think of any baby animals that use their moms as rafts in the water? (otters, walruses, swans, alligators)

◆ How do chimps, gorillas, and monkeys carry their babies? (in their arms, on their backs)

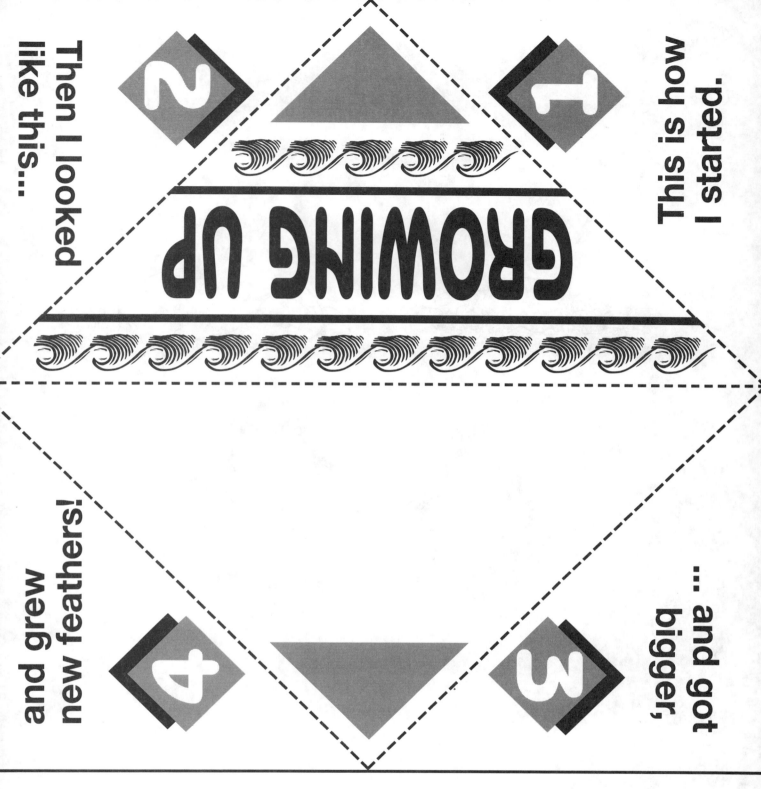

Then I looked like this...

2

1

This is how I started.

GROWING UP

... and got bigger,

3

and grew new feathers!

4

✂ Cut along the solid line above.

EMPEROR FOR A DAY

Do you know why some penguins don't build nests? There's nothing to build them with! No twigs, no weeds, no grass, no leaves.... Yet eggs have to be kept warm in order to hatch, so Emperor penguins use their own feet as nests! Shortly after she lays her egg, the female returns to the sea. The father penguin carefully rolls the egg onto the top of his feet and tucks it under a warm flap of skin on his belly, called a brood patch. He shuffles around with the egg like that for two whole months until the egg hatches.

Try to do what an Emperor penguin does!

1. Form an egg shape, using one can of Play-Doh™ (or a school-made substitute).

2. Remove your shoes but leave your socks on.

3. Carefully balance the egg across the top of your feet. (To keep it there, you'll have to curl your toes up.)

4. See if you can shuffle-walk across the room and back without letting the egg roll off your feet!

1. Was carrying the egg on your feet harder or easier than you thought it would be?_____

2. Describe what happened when you tried._____
_____

3. What does the Emperor penguin have that makes it easier for him than for you?_____

4. What might make it harder for him?_____

_____

Penguins on the Move

Where Penguins Live

Although we tend to think of ice and snow when we think of penguins, only the Emperor, Adélie, and Chinstrap are exclusively Antarctic. More penguin species live in somewhat milder climates on sub-Antarctic islands, such as the Falklands and South Georgia. Others live along the coasts of South Africa, South America, Australia, and New Zealand. And the Galápagos penguin lives just a few miles from the Equator! (The common factor is cold water, which occurs close to the Equator near South America.) While most of the more tropical species feed quite close to their nesting grounds (because not far away, the ocean becomes too warm), the less tropical ones may travel as far as 200 miles to their feeding areas, staying at sea for months at a time. Young penguins are at sea for the first one or two years of their lives!

How Penguins Swim

In water, penguins may swim slowly on the surface, but submerge when they need to increase their speed. In order to take breaths of air without slowing, they burst from the water in a motion called porpoising. This same thrust is what propels penguins out of the water and onto ice or land in spectacular exit leaps. Of course, sometimes they just walk from the sea up the beach, like we do. Because most of the smaller penguins feed fairly close to the surface, their dives aren't very deep or prolonged. The larger species are another matter—they like to eat krill and squid, and that means deeper dives. Emperor and King penguins are capable of diving to depths of nearly 900 feet and have been known to stay down for almost 20 minutes! As graceful as they are in water, penguins appear comical and awkward on land. (Famous bird authority Roger Tory Peterson once described them as "animated laundry bags.") Their feet are set far back on their bodies, which causes them to stand in a more upright position than other birds, and their plump bodies and stiff wings have led us to describe their gait as waddling. In soft snow, though, these waddlers can outrun a person! Penguins also get around by hopping and tobogganing, shown on the following pages.

PLACING THE FACE:

The project on pages 35 to 37 invites students to explore a map. Duplicate and distribute the three pages to the children. Have them cut out both parts of the Southern Hemisphere map and tape or paste them together. (To give children a clearer concept of the southern hemisphere, show them how the same area appears on a globe.) After students find out where each species lives by checking the habitat information on the Penguin Profile Cards, they can cut out the penguin squares and paste them in the proper places on their maps.

Extension Activity:

Try any of the following discussion starters to help students discover more about habitats.

◆ What's the closest penguins come to living near us? (Galápagos)

◆ Water is one of the most important considerations with respect to where a penguin lives. What's important about the places we live? Why?

◆ Can you think of reasons scientists might take penguins away from the places they live? (Endangered species can be bred and returned to their habitats. Penguins whose habitats are destroyed can be relocated to more environmentally safe places.)

PENGUIN WATER WHEEL:

The wheels on page 38 show penguins in water activities. Make copies, distribute them to your students, and help them assemble the wheels according to the directions that follow. To assemble the wheels:

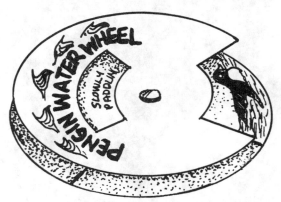

1. Cut the wheels out along the dark lines and use a hole punch to make the center holes. Make sure to cut out the windows in wheel A.

2. Place wheel A on top of wheel B and attach them with a brass fastener.

After children have looked at their wheels, you might want to explain the pictures more thoroughly, covering the following points:

◆ Groups of penguins gather at the edge of the ice and jostle one another until several are bumped in. The others follow unless one of the first penguins is attacked by a leopard seal. The Adélies shown aren't deep underwater divers (they dive about 300 feet), but when Emperors hunt for squid, they often dive nearly 900 feet and stay submerged for almost 20 minutes!

◆ Penguins move slowly when they're on the surface. They use their flippers to paddle instead of using their feet like ducks do.

◆ The porpoise-like leap out of the water and in again is a way for penguins to get a breath of air without substantially slowing their speed. Using a burst of energy and speed, penguins seem to pop out of the water onto the shore (or ice). These quick exits often help them escape from orcas and seals.

MOVING ON LAND, SNOW, AND ICE:

By comparing a penguin to a bird they are familiar with, your students can get a better grasp of the penguins' unique structural adaptations. When they study the legs and feet of both birds, the children will understand the abilities and limitations of the two birds. Reproduce and distribute page 39 to each student. After students have completed the sheet, you might want to expand on avian form and function by asking questions like: Why do hummingbirds have such long bills? (to reach into trumpet shaped flowers) Why do ducks have webbed feet? (they make better water paddles) Why do eagles have such powerful talons? (for grabbing prey), and so on.

POPSICLE PAL PUPPET:

On pages 40 and 41 you will find directions and an easy four-piece pattern for making a penguin puppet with moveable flippers and feet. After distributing copies of each page to your students, ask them to paste the pattern sheets to cardboard and color their penguins so that they look like one of the species in the illustrations: Chinstrap, Adélie, or Galápagos. After coloring, help them cut and assemble the puppets. To create a "habitat," students can use colored paper or painted cardboard to look like ice, snow, or rocky shores. Children can then pretend their penguins are waddling or hopping, and may enjoy adding sound effects like braying and squawking to the birds' motions.

PLACING THE FACE

Did you know that there are no penguins at the North Pole? That's because they all live in the Southern Hemisphere.

If you hold a globe of the world above your head and look up, you'll see the part of the earth where penguins live. The map on pages 36 and 37 is of the "penguin half of the world."

What You Do

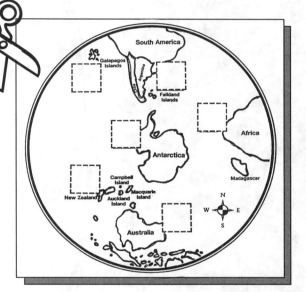

1. Cut out both parts of the map and paste them on poster board so they line up properly.

2. Cut out the six penguin squares.

3. Find out where each species lives by looking at your Penguin Profile Cards.

4. Find those places on your map and paste each penguin in its own habitat.

When you're finished making your map, answer these questions:

Which penguin lives furthest north?_____

Which penguin lives off the New Zealand coast?_____

Do any penguins live on Madagascar?_____

Which penguin lives furthest south?_____

Which penguin lives on the Australian coast?_____

YELLOW-EYED

AFRICAN

EMPEROR

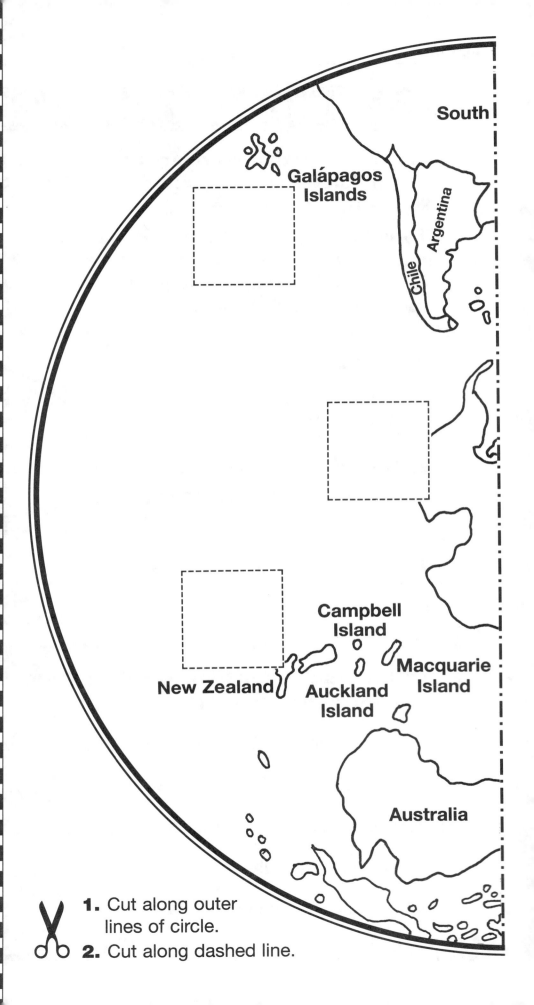

South

Galápagos
Islands

Chile

Argentina

Campbell
Island

New Zealand

Auckland
Island

Macquarie
Island

Australia

1. Cut along outer
lines of circle.

2. Cut along dashed line.

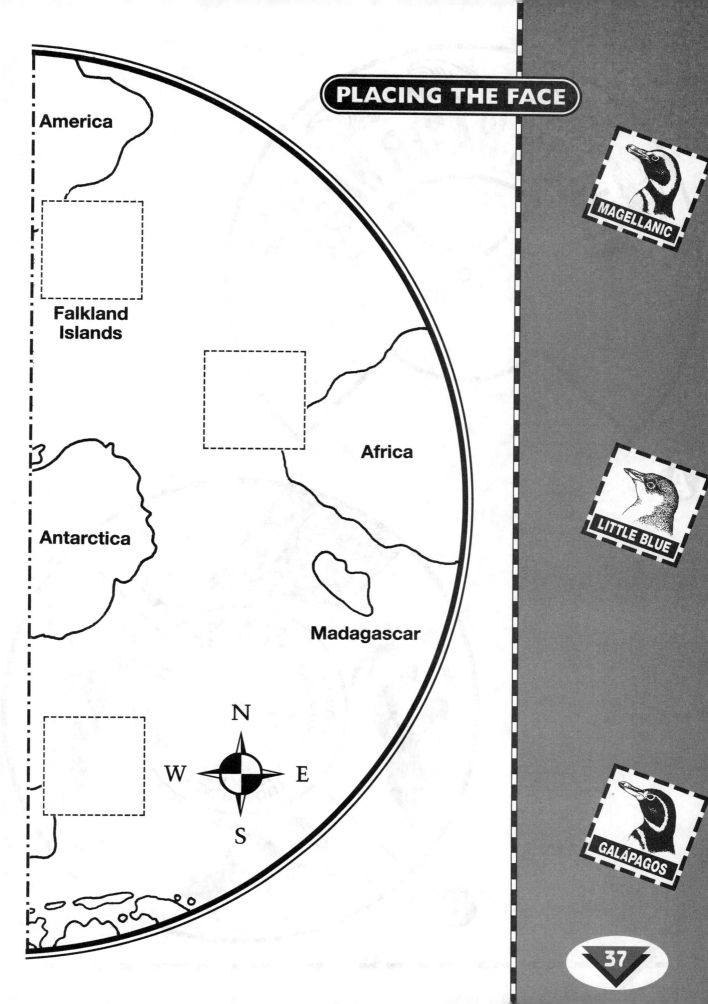

America

Falkland
Islands

Africa

Antarctica

Madagascar

N
W   E
S

MAGELLANIC

LITTLE BLUE

GALÁPAGOS

PENGUIN WATER WHEEL

A

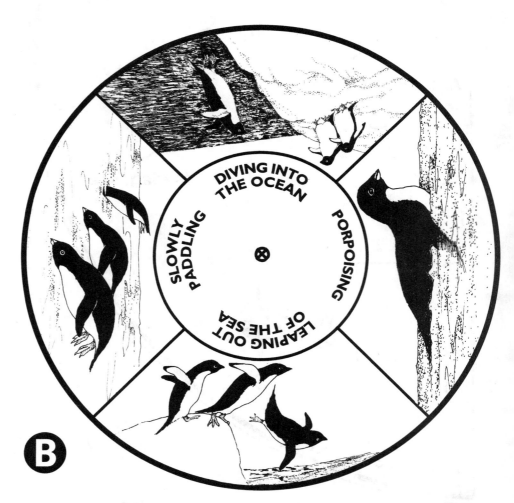

DIVING INTO THE OCEAN

PORPOISING

LEAPING OUT OF THE SEA

SLOWLY PADDLING

B

Name _____

Compare a penguin with a bird you see often, such as a sparrow. (Look carefully at its legs and feet.)

1. Which bird stands up straighter?_____

2. Are the legs of both birds in the same place on the body?

_____

3. What might happen if the penguin leaned forward like the sparrow?

_____

4. Describe the shape of both birds' feet.

_____

5. Why do you think a penguin's feet might move better on ice than a sparrow's feet?

_____

6. Sparrows can't toboggan like the penguins below. What might get in their way if they tried?

_____

POPSICLE PAL PUPPET

You can make a puppet that will waddle and waggle. Look at the pictures below and decide if you want your puppet to be an Adélie, a Chinstrap, or a Galápagos penguin. Use the picture as a guide and color your penguin so it looks like your favorite one. And don't forget to color the edges of the wings!

What You Need:

- ◆ strong tape
- ◆ cardboard
- ◆ black crayon or marker
- ◆ craft stick
- ◆ scissors
- ◆ glue

ADÉLIE

CHINSTRAP

GALÁPAGOS

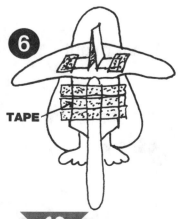

What You Do:

1. Glue the pattern to the cardboard and color the penguin.

2. Cut out the four shapes along the solid lines.

3. Place the penguin face down. Locate the flipper/feet piece so that the feet are just a little bit lower than the body.

4. Tape part A down on both sides as shown in the illustration.

5. Fold the action tab, part B, on the dotted lines and tape it to the wing section as shown.

6. Attach the craft stick to part A with three pieces of tape.

7. Your Popsicle Pal is finished! Move the tab from side to side and watch your penguin move its flippers and feet!

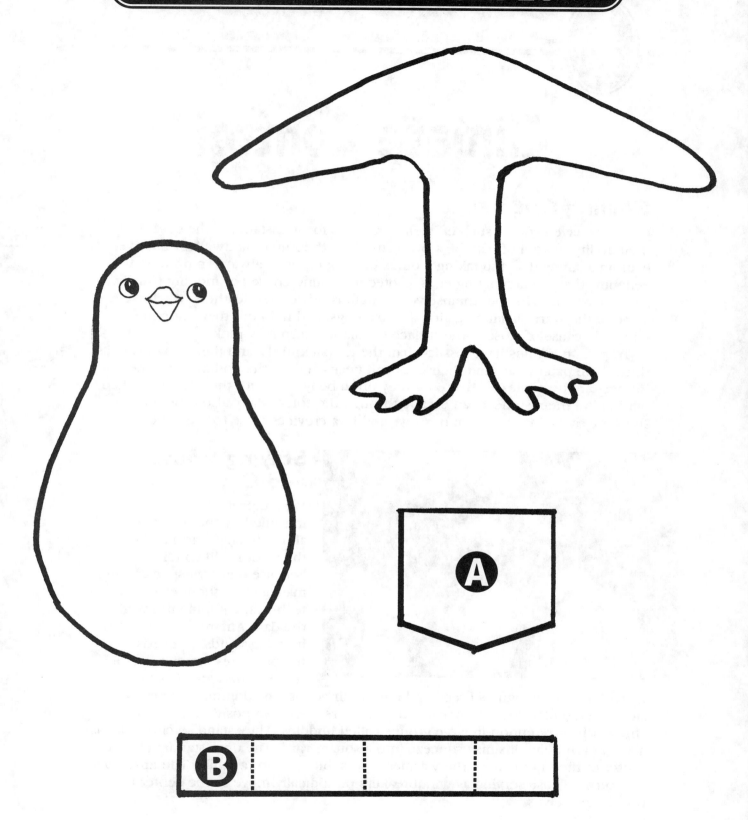

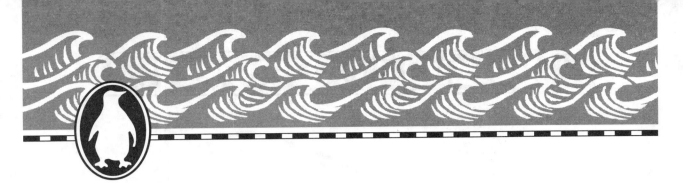

Climate Control

Chilling Out

Penguins have evolved such efficient strategies for withstanding the cold that their ability to cool off can be a problem. Even the Antarctic dwellers can overheat on a sunny day, and taking a quick cooling dip isn't always an option. Penguins that are incubating eggs, protecting young chicks, or molting usually have to stay put. To cool themselves, penguins ruffle their feathers to release some of the warm insulating air, pant like dogs, and hold out their flippers which, because of close-to-the-surface capillaries, turn rosy pink.

Tropical penguins have less fat than the ice-pack birds, and their down isn't as thick. Bare patches around their eyes and beaks and on the underside of their flippers are heat-release areas, and they often belly-flop with their feet stretched out behind them so heat can escape through the soles. Many also avoid bright sunshine by taking shelter in burrows and lava crevices close to the water.

Staying Warm and Dry

We are probably more intrigued by the penguin's ability to stay warm and dry in the most frigid conditions because our own species can't manage it without elaborate technical equipment! Imagine the dark Antarctic winter with howling winds, blizzards, and temperatures far icier than any we've experienced—and that's when Emperor penguins breed and raise their young. In addition to their layer of fat, a thick undercoat, and dense outer feathers, they also position themselves for efficient heat retention in large groups called huddles. They stand so close that as many as ten penguins may squeeze into a square yard! The ones standing in the center of the huddle have the warmest spots, but only for a while. The Emperors take turns. Those serving as windbreakers periodically move to the center to warm themselves.

COZY IN THE COLD:

The experiment on page 44 demonstrates the insulation properties of air. In previous chapters we've mentioned that the thick layer of down next to the penguin's skin is what traps air and, consequently, body heat. Using three small zip-lock plastic bags, one of which contains ice cubes and water, your students can feel for themselves how a buffer of air protects their hands from the cold. The experiment can be performed in small groups, with the children taking turns.

Extension Activity:

Challenge children to design their own insulating devices to protect their hands from the bag with ice, then perform experiments to test their ideas (or put together presentations explaining how their devices work). Compare the new insulators with the air bags. Follow up by brainstorming all the ways people protect themselves from the cold (different kinds of clothing, blankets, windows, curtains, furnaces, wood stoves, insulation, solar heat systems, and so on), Ask: *How do other animals cope with the cold?* Discuss ways some animals adapt to the cold, for example, by building up layers of fat, by hibernating, or by migrating to a warmer place!

DRENCHED AND DRY:

When a cat gets wet, it really gets wet—right down to the skin. But when a penguin pops out of the sea, a few shakes gets the water off its feathers. The activity on pages 45 and 46 explains how waterproofing works and asks the children to waterproof a penguin with crayons. They'll be able to see why penguins don't get soaked, and why cats do.

Extension Activity:

Talk about why cats don't have the same protective coating that penguins do. Ask: *Do cats need to spend time in cool water gathering food? What do we use to stay dry when it rains?* Invite students to suggest protective features cats have that penguins don't need (for example, claws to help them climb). Investigate other protective features of different animals, such as porcupines' quills.

COZY IN THE COLD

How do penguins stay warm? Underneath their sleek top feathers, right against their skin, is a layer of downy feathers (like the soft ones in a pillow) that traps air. The air keeps body heat in and cold air out. **See for yourself!**

What You Need:
◆ three small zip-lock plastic bags
◆ cold water and ice

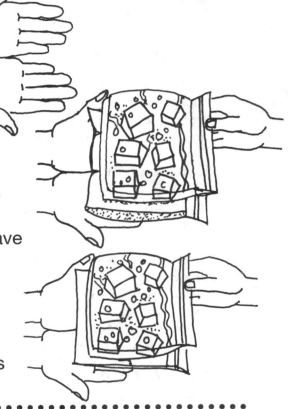

What You Do:
1. Fill one bag about half way with cold water and ice cubes. Close the bag completely!

2. Zip a second bag most of the way. Blow air into the small gap and zip it up quickly. It should be like an air pillow.

3. Hold your hands together, palms up. Have a classmate place the air bag on your palms, and then put the ice bag on top.

4. Now have your helper replace the air bag with the empty flat bag, and put the ice bag on top of it.

5. Take turns! Help one of your classmates with the experiment.

1. Which bag kept the cold out better, the empty one or the air bag?

_____

2. Can you think of something else that would do a better job of protecting your hands from the ice bag?

_____

3. Some people like to wear several layers of clothing when they are in the cold. Why do you think this would help keep them warm?

_____

DRENCHED AND DRY

Do you remember why penguins don't get cold and soaked to the skin when they swim?

Air trapped in their down keeps cold out, and outer feathers that overlap like tightly fitted roof tiles keep the water out. Those outer feathers are waxy, too. Penguins spend a lot of time applying wax to their outer feathers. The wax comes from a gland at the base of their tail. They use their beak to apply it. To find out how waxy feathers help penguins, try the following activity.

Color the penguin on the next page with crayons (which are waxy!), but don't color the cat. Make sure you thoroughly color every bit of the penguin, even the white part.

After you finish coloring, dip your fingers in water and sprinkle some on the penguin and some on the cat. Hold the page up and watch what happens!

1. What happened to the penguin when you sprinkled it with water?

_____

2. Can you think of other birds whose feathers shed water?

_____

3. What happened to the cat when you sprinkled it with water?

_____

4. Why do you think most cats don't like water?

_____

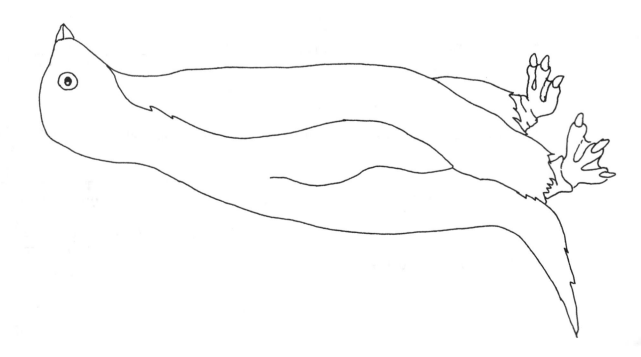

DRENCHED AND DRY

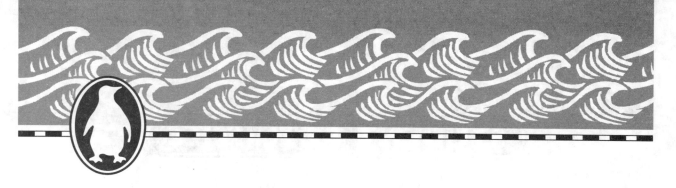

Getting Along

Danger!

Most penguins are colonial birds, spending their time both at sea and on land in large noisy groups, or flocks. Often, more than one species inhabit the same area: Adélies and Emperors both breed far south on Antarctica; the Falkland Islands are home to Rockhoppers, as well as some Kings and Gentoos. Many of the temperate penguins share sites with entirely different species: cormorants, gulls, pelicans, steamer ducks, and elephant seals. Galápagos penguins share space with marine iguanas and scarlet crabs, and both Yellow-Eyed penguins and rabbits inhabit Enderby island.

Danger is always imminent. Large gulls called skuas hover above penguin colonies, waiting to grab unguarded eggs and chicks. In the sea, penguins are potential meals for leopard seals (see picture at right), orcas (killer whales), and sharks. But although those predators take a heavy toll on the penguin population, that toll is insignificant compared to the dangers presented by people.

Not all penguin habitats are pristine and inaccessible to people. Some have been severely damaged by commercial fishing. Others are destroyed when guano (sea bird excrement that penguins use for nesting) is collected for fertilizer. Egging (when people take eggs for food) continues to be a problem for South American and African penguin species. King penguins are still recovering from being overhunted for their oil, produced by boiling their bodies to remove the fat. (Less than 200 years ago, a famous explorer reported having killed 3,000 penguins in one day!) Oil spilled from ships not only destroys habitats but dissolves penguins' waxy coatings and mats their down, allowing cold water to reach their skin. The penguins then die from loss of body heat. Another difficult problem to solve is that humans take too many fish from the sea, depleting penguins' food supply.

Protecting Penguins

The up side is that there are now laws protecting penguins, and scientists are trying to establish new colonies of endangered penguins by hand-rearing chicks on environmentally safe sites. Efforts are also being made to restore nesting areas on the Australian islands once lost to sheep ranching, and the result is that the affected penguins are increasing in number.

ESCAPE!

The maze on page 49 asks your students to help an Adélie penguin find its way across broken ice to the safety of a snowy coast. While students have fun working out the route, they'll reinforce their understanding of penguins' habitats and major predators.

Name

ESCAPE!

Help this Adélie penguin cross the ice maze and get to its colony. (Be careful! There are leopard seals lurking in the water who would like to have a penguin snack!) Look at the different ice paths and figure out which way the penguin should go. Mark the safe route with a crayon.

Researching Penguins

Gathering Information

While much information can be gathered from observing captive animals under controlled conditions, many biologists find that studying animals in their natural habitat is more satisfying, more challenging, and on many levels, more accurate. But observing penguins in the Antarctic isn't easy.

When David Ainley and other biologists from P.R.B.O. International Biological Research go to the Antarctic, they travel by plane or ship (ice-breaker). Once they reach the supply station, they switch to helicopter, tracked vehicle, or inflatable boat, depending on the site. Their work, and the ships, aircraft, and vehicles, are part of the U.S. Antarctic Program (of the National Science Foundation).

Since identifying individual birds is essential to understanding their behavior, one of the first jobs is putting numbered bands or rings on the penguins' flippers. This can be done in about 20 seconds and is harmless to the penguins. The Adélie penguins ignore the scientists until they come closer than 30 feet. But even then they don't flee. "To an Adélie," Dr. Ainley said, "a human is probably like a large Emperor penguin."

The biologists band most birds as chicks in the crèche (a group of juveniles) by herding them into a sheep pen. Some adults are banded as they sit on their eggs (scientists do this by covering the penguin's eyes with one hand and slipping the band on with the other). Other penguins are caught with a hand-net so they can be banded and then let go.

In some of the earlier studies, biologists were trying to learn about the Adélies' social behavior, and were also trying to compare the migratory Adélies, which nest closely in a big group, with Yellow-Eyed penguins, a more solitary species that doesn't travel far. The scientists compared breeding success and life spans of the two species. And they found answers to some of their questions: Do Adélies return to breed near to where they were born? (yes) What do they eat? (fish and krill) How far do they travel to find food? (up to 45 miles) How long does the trip take? (three days on average) Do Adélies eat the same things in winter and summer? (no, they eat more fish in winter) Do Adélies mate for life? (not really; they need to return to their breeding site in sync; if they are out of phase with one another, a new mate is usually chosen) In contrast, the Yellow-Eyed penguins, though they breed close to where they hatched, eat mostly fish; travel only a few hours and a few miles for food; and mate for life.

Questions and Answers

Dr. Ainley and his group are now trying to understand why penguin populations are increasing in the Ross Sea area. They theorize it has to do with global warming, which results in less pack ice. With less ice, the Adélies can get from their colonies to their feeding areas faster (because instead of making their way slowly over ice, they can swim rapidly in open water), and get more food to their chicks. This means fatter chicks with a higher survival rate.

Although scientists may find answers to the questions they started with, inevitably still more questions arise. There is always more to discover and understand, and marine biologists still have to solve the mysteries of what penguins do when they are in the sea.

PENGUIN FIELD STUDY

Before starting the Penguin Field Study, distribute strips of construction paper to be made into "flipper" ID bands, and assign a number for each band. Ask the children to make some penguin sounds like braying, squawking, quacking, babbling, honking, and peeping. Then talk about some things penguins do when they're out of the water—waddling, shuffling, hopping (as ways of getting around); flipper-tapping (used in courtship); pecking (used in defense of their space); and head-bowing (used in greeting). Invite children to try these actions.

Next divide the class in half, distributing photocopies of pages 53 and 54 to all students. One half will be field biologists and the other half will pretend to be a colony of penguins with the numbered ID bands on their "flippers" (arms). The "penguins" will act out the motions and sounds discussed above, while the "biologists" fill in a data chart to record their observations. After about five to ten minutes, the groups can switch roles. When students have completed their data sheets, they can total their observations and color in the columns to form bar graphs.

Extension Activity:

Invite students to share their experiences as field biologists and to compare the results of their studies. The following questions can help guide your discussion.

◆ Which behavior was observed most often? Least often? Invite students to suggest reasons for these results.

◆ What kinds of things can influence results of a study like this? For instance, do you think you observed and recorded all examples of all behaviors?

◆ If you were researching penguins, would you study them in captivity or in their natural habitats? Encourage students to discuss this question. For example, penguins in captivity may not behave the way they do in their natural habitats, but when penguins are in the sea, it is difficult to observe what they're doing.

PENGUIN FIELD STUDY

Read the names of the columns across the bottom of the field study chart. When you see a penguin do any of the things listed, enter its identification number in a rectangle, starting from the bottom and working up. When your observation time is over, color each space that has an ID number written in it.

Using the left side of the chart you can read the total of how many times you saw each activity.

1. How many penguins flipper-tapped? _____

2. Did you see more penguins waddle than hop? _____

3. How many different penguins made noise? _____

4. Did more penguins shuffle than head-bow? _____

5. What behavior did you see the least? _____

6. What did penguins do the most? _____

7. Did more penguins peck or make noise? _____

PENGUIN FIELD STUDY

	10						
9							
8							
7							
6							
5							
4							
3							
2							
1							
	Hop	Shuffle Walk	Waddle Walk	Flipper Tap	Head Bow	Make Noise	Peck

Glossary

Antarctica: the region around the South Pole

blubber: a layer of fat under the skin

boldest: bravest, most daring

bray: to make a loud sound like a donkey

brood patch: a fold of the flesh on a penguin's lower belly, used to keep eggs and chicks warm

burrow: to make a hole

coastal: land area along the ocean

colonies: groups of animals living close together

crown: the top of the head

down: fine soft feathers

dunes: low sand hills

endangered: in danger of becoming extinct

Equator: on maps, the imaginary line around the earth that divides the Northern and Southern Hemispheres

flippers: limbs of an animal; the penguin's wings

habitat: a special area in which a species finds its food and shelter

incubate: keep eggs warm until they hatch

krill: small, shrimp-like animals

leopard seal: a large spotted sea mammal that eats penguins (and other prey)

lurking: waiting while hidden

marine iguana: algae-eating, swimming lizard of the Galápagos

molted: in birds, to have shed its feathers

orca: a killer whale

peninsula: a "finger" of land surrounded on three sides by water

plume: a group of long feathers

porpoising: "swim-leaping" like porpoises

rudder: something used for steering

shuffle: to walk without lifting the feet

sleek: smooth

soar: to ride or fly through the air

soles: the bottoms of the feet

spines: thorn-like shapes that line penguins' bills and tongues

squid: a sea animal related to the octopus

Suggested Reading

For Students:

Austen, E. *Birds That Stopped Flying* (Random House, 1969)

Bonner, S. *A Penguin Year* (Delacorte Press, 1980)

Crow, S. L. *Penguins and Polar Bears* (National Geographic Society, 1985)

Johnson, S. *Penguins* (Lerner Publication, 1981)

Penney, R. *The Penguins Are Coming* (HarperCollins, 1969)

Somme, L. & Kalas, S. *The Penguin Family* (Picture Book Studio, 1988)

Strange, I. J. *Penguin World* (Dodd Mead, 1981)

For Teachers:

Ainley, D.G., R.E. LeRashe & W.J.L. Sladen. *The Breeding Biology of the Adélie Penguin* (University of California Press, 1983)

Naven, Ron et al. *Wild Ice* Antarctic Journeys (Smithsonian, 1990)

Peterson, Roger Tory. *Penguins* (Houghton Mifflin, 1979)

Answers

PENGUIN FRIENDS (page 13)
1. The markings under its chin looks like a chinstrap
2. white rings
3. Little Blue
4. its head feathers
5. black stripe
6. responses will vary

STAND UP BIRDS (page 24)
1. Gentoo
2. 6
3. 30
4. Adélie
5. Magellanic, Adélie, Chinstrap, Royal
6. responses will vary
7. responses will vary

EMPEROR FOR A DAY (page 31)
1. responses will vary
2. responses will vary
3. brood patch to help hold egg in place
4. walking on ice, strong winds, snow

PLACING THE FACE (page 35)
1. Galápagos
2. Yellow-Eyed
3. no
4. Emperor
5. Little Blue

MOVING ON LAND, SNOW, AND ICE (page 39)
1. penguin
2. no; penguin's legs are set far back
3. it would topple on its face
4. penguin's feet are thick; sparrow's feet are thin
5. they have more gripping surface and stronger nails
6. their feet

COZY IN THE COLD (page 44)
1. air bag
2. responses will vary
3. air is trapped between layers

DRENCHED AND DRY (page 45)
1. water rolled off penguin
2. pelicans, ducks, geese, gulls (water birds)
3. soaked in
4. they get wet to the skin

ESCAPE! (page 49)